I've Been There...
I Feel Your Pain

I've Been There...
I Feel Your Pain

—eWw—

I've Been There...I Feel Your Pain
Copyright © 2019 by eWw

Library of Congress Control Number: 2019914713
ISBN-13:   Paperback: 978-1-950073-83-2
              ePub: 978-1-950073-84-9

All rights reserved. No part of this publication may be reproduced, distributed, or transmitted in any form or by any means, including photocopying, recording, or other electronic or mechanical methods, without the prior written permission of the publisher or author, except in the case of brief quotations embodied in critical reviews and certain other noncommercial uses permitted by copyright law.

Although every precaution has been taken to verify the accuracy of the information contained herein, the author and publisher assume no responsibility for any errors or omissions. No liability is assumed for damages that may result from the use of information contained within.

Printed in the United States of America

GoToPublish LLC
1-888-337-1724
www.gotopublish.com
info@gotopublish.com

This book was written on true accounts, twenty-six years ago in the life of my children and I, which I now dedicate to them with all my love:

Keda – My oldest daughter

Peanut – My son

Cece – My babygirl who didn't make it

Without you all, I wouldn't be the person I am today and for the experience and the hand of God, my creator – who kept me during those trying times.

Thank You Father for Loving Me!!!

I've Been There . . . . I Feel Your Pain

I use to wonder what was going through a person's mind just at that moment when nothing else mattered, no one else cared, just you and your fate looking at each other face to face and then . . . .

At age 13, my older sister and I shared a room together. We were already bedded down for the night, but suddenly, awakened by a disturbance in the next room occupied by our parents. As we looked at each other trying to figure out what was going on, the next thing we heard will echo in my ears for the rest of my life. Not knowing then that this would be the turning point of my life, and subconsciously, the decisions made from that point on would be based on those words that were spoken in so much anger; which has always sent chills down my spine. Who would have thought

that from this day forward, my life would take such a drastic change?

One of the things that sticks close to mind in my upbringing, was to look for good in every person or situation. Sometimes even this seemed hard to do when the good was buried so deep inside. I took pride in treating people the way I wanted to be treated and give them the benefit of the doubt; which meant, loving unconditionally, looking past all faults, and accepting individuals totally as a whole. As years passed, I was taught to love everybody and separate their acts.

This became a welcomed challenge for me. I can remember times when through associating with my childhood friends, there were other kids that seemed to stand out to them, and for some reason my associates chose not to have any dealings with them. They were considered, in their eyes, as outcasts for some reason or another; they weren't liked. It could have been because of the way they dressed, or they had a flaw in their appearance, or any number of reasons. There was always a sadness in my heart for them.

I found myself extending to them friendship and looking for the goodness in them that no one else wanted to find, and before I knew it, they began to put forth an effort to meet me half way.

I can also remember during these days, my tolerance level was at its peak. Endurance was my middle name.

I believed that being honest with those you came in contact with would eliminate second guesses, and provide a sense of security for those with whom you have dealings.

During my childhood days, I became very competitive. Striving to prove I was someone special, and I needed love like anybody else. I craved affection and approval. I wanted my family and friends to like me, love me, and accept me.

What I heard that night still brings tears to my eyes as I'm living out my adult life. I heard the voice of the man whom I thought was my father—my biological father, the man I trusted and respected, deny my existence and his part in my life. The only father image I've known and loved say "I wasn't his" . . . I never did understand why I was treated so differently than the way my other sister and brother were treated. I felt like I didn't belong, like an outsider, and nobody loved me or cared for me. I kept asking myself "What was wrong with me?", "Why can't I be loved?", "What was I to do?"

Now, here I was feeling like an outcast. No sense of belonging. Do you know what that feels like when you can't connect or associate with a person, place or thing? You just exist minute to minute.

I've Been There...I Feel Your Pain

My self esteem was diminishing; no motivation. I started disliking myself, constantly wondering what did I do wrong? Can't they still love me?

I cried myself to sleep many nights, while thinking how I could please them tomorrow? How could I keep them from being upset with me? I maintained good academic grades in school. I did my household chores with extra effort, always seeking praise or some kind of positive reaction. But for some reason, that didn't come. I had so much love to give, but no one seemed to want it. This love stayed bottled up inside me. I felt like I was going to burst!!!

After several more years of my parents' heated discussions and a 25th wedding anniversary, my only known parents were graced with a divorce. There was some signs of relief for me. I always felt that I was responsible for the disturbances and if it were not for me, they wouldn't be together. It was as though a burden was lifted off my shoulders. I didn't have to carry the guilt of their being married because of me anymore.

It was during this time that I met a boy, graduated, attended college, and got married. Almost immediately, I wanted to have a family. I guess we were trying so hard, but nothing seem to work. We saw doctor after doctor but still, to no avail. I became very frustrated and just gave up on the idea.

After two (2) years of marriage, I became pregnant, but due to complications lost my child. She was born prematurely, developed complications and died seventeen days later. She was a little fighter at one pound five ounces. I guess her little heart couldn't take the stress, she gave up. This was the first time I was able to express love in a way I hadn't been able to before. This seemed harder than I thought because, here again, I was looking for acceptance and security. Problems began to set in with my husband and I, and unbeknowing to us both. I became pregnant again. Prematurely, our child was born. A beautiful little girl.

I had made up my mind that this child would know what being loved meant. My husband and I could not resolve the problems we were experiencing, and I felt I was literally raising our child alone. So I decided it was time to move on, that this was not the environment in which I wanted our child to be raised in.

Two and a half years later, I found myself in the middle of a divorce with threats on my life and that of my family. I noticed also, that with my child's development, she began to require more affection than I knew how to give. The material things in life didn't seem to be enough. She required more physical attention. How could I supply her with this when I wasn't held lovingly? I tried so hard, but with being a single parent and trying to raise my child by satisfying all of her needs, it was difficult.

For another couple of years, I vowed to raise my child alone. I didn't want the benefit or the comfort of another man. It frightened me in many ways. Rejection was not an easy thing to stomach. I couldn't understand or figure out why it would drain me so with involvements. I seemed to pour everything I had into these situations only to be rejected, and left with feelings of being used. It seemed as though as soon as I would let me guard down enough to express an interest, or get attached to someone, they failed me.

I needed someone to talk to, someone to help me figure these feelings out. I had no close friend, no adult figure to guide me. I began to keep things closed up inside me. I dealt with things the best way I knew how.

Yes, with my constant fear of being alone or lonely, I met another. I thought that just having someone close to me, and being able to reach out and touch him when I felt lonely, that this would help fill the void in my personal and physical life. I justified this as being better than nothing at all.

After approximately five years into this new relationship, I again found myself pregnant. This time, with a bouncing baby boy. Boy—did things start going downhill! First of all, he didn't want a child. Now, what was I supposed to do? Well, after my son was born, but not without more medical complications, at one point a decision was being discussed as to who the doctors were more concerned about. My baby was going through stress and the doctors didn't believe he would survive delivery.

I tried to make the current situation work out for another two years. Things just got worse. I couldn't work by order of my doctor. I was in and out of the hospital. He didn't want to fully support us. He went through very strange mood changes. Started drinking more and more, and eventually lost his job. Due to my high risk status, I became eligible for government assistance, where my medical bills were taken care of in addition to other services. He began threatening me and became violent. Coupled with his drinking; I became a basket case. I couldn't sleep at nights, I was scared to close my eyes. He seemed to get joy out of my fear. I began to pray, I mean pray without ceasing. I knew that if I was going to get out of this alive, the Lord had to take control, if not for my safety, for the safety of my children. I kept my friends and family away. I didn't know what he was going to do . . . eventually, I was removed out of that situation.

A decision was going to have to be made either to take the baby or lose me. Well, this baby made the decision for us, it was coming, again prematurely. It was also at this time, that my mother's medical problems increased. I believe stress I was going through became very stressful for her too. Here again, I began to wonder if I was responsible for her unhappiness and inflamed medical condition.

On one occasion when my mother and I were home alone, I thought the mood was right, I asked mom who my father was. If you could have seen the look on her face as I uttered those words, you would think I had just snatched her last breath. That was a subject I never brought up again. Four months after my son's birth, she passed away. This was the only person whom I felt could answer those questions that continue to eat at me. Who was my father? Was he still alive? Did he love me? Had he tried to see me or contact me? Why? Now these answers went with her to her grave.

Now, even with two children to raise, one would think that should be enough. Sure they kept me hoping but still there was something missing . . .

After God's intervention in my last involvement, I sought refuge in the church. The experiences and growth which was manifested seemed to fill the void left in my heart and my life. I truly believe I'm a child of God's and he watches over me always. I also believe that we can interfere in God's plan and deter or delay our blessings by the choices we make. But he's so good and just that he forgives us, picks us up, dusts us off and places our feet on solid ground again, and again. I know I'm not where I need to be in Christ. I know what my weaknesses are which make temptations hard to fight off. The lack of physical attention like being held, touched tenderly, kissed compassionately and being cared for, cared about and needed are all still strong desires.

It seems to always go back to those feelings of not belonging. The need to know there's a place for me somewhere and in that place someone who could love me.

I've Been There...I Feel Your Pain

I should have stopped here!! If I hadn't met the guy yet that could provide me with the desires of my heart out of love, I should have known, it wasn't going to happen.

It seemed with each involvement, a little piece of me was ripped away leaving unhealable scars. Now don't get me wrong, I know life is filled with ups and downs and with these ups and downs, we grow, learn, and mature. Nor could I began to know what anyone else may have gone through and the affect it played in their life. I can only speak of me and what I've experienced. I'm on the inside looking out.

There must be something, something I'm overlooking. Something I'm doing wrong. Something that I'm doing that would cause the same reactions. But what?

Why did it always appear I led a trail to all the undesireables in my life? It always appeared I brought the worst side out in them. Did I become that vulnerable and magnetized that I radiated vibes of saying "here I am world take a shot". "While you are at it, use me. I have no feelings".

Well, in this next situation I was targeted. Not beknowing to me, but being vulnerable, there were certain safety checks that went omitted. He was a controlling companion. A take charge person. Very dominating. He appeared genuinely concerned about my children and my welfare. As time passed, he became more dominating and alienated me from my family and friends. He made me feel guilty about the positive things in my life. My church, my having female friends, I could do nothing right. I started questioning this relationship in my mind. I knew something was wrong, but I couldn't pin point what it was.

I've Been There...I Feel Your Pain

It was around this time that I started having problems with my daughter. Problems like acting out, defiance, attitude change. I started forms of punishment, he seemed to undermine my authority with her. He had developed this weird questionable relationship with her. When she and I were alone, I would ask, what I thought were the appropriate questions. Either she had no answer or just plainly denied anything was going on. She never questioned, implied, or stated she was in anyway afraid, needed my help or needed help of any kind.

I continued to pray for my family. I knew in my heart something was not right. I just couldn't figure out what it was.

Shortly there after, I was contacted at work by the authorities at my daughter's school. I was told that my daughter was in custody there and they needed me to come. I tried to get a line on what the problem was but they were closed mouth and would not divulge any information. I just thought that because of my daughter's attitude problems of late, she had acted out in school.

Being that I shared this car with my friend and we commuted back and forth to work together, he was notified that I needed to get to my daughter's school.

After our arrival, somehow we were separated. I was taken into where my daughter was. Also seated there were the guidance counselor and a representative from the police department. My daughter sat silently, watching my every emotion. What then transpired is a mother's worst nightmare. For a couple of years, my daughter had been putting up with abuse from this man. Initially, touching inappropriately to fondling to actual rape. At this point she had had enough of this threats of hurting me and his blackmail of anything she had done that I wouldn't approve of that he had kept as a secret between the two of them.

I became so disoriented, I didn't know where I was or who they were talking about. I couldn't figure out how this was happening under my roof. My daughter and I had a system, upon her leaving in the mornings and arriving home in the afternoons. She would call me. I would call her upon arriving at work. The acts took place after contacts so that I wouldn't detect any problems. Since my place of employment was out of the city in which we resided, it would take a while to get to either locations. There were unexplained times when he would suggest I either take the bus to work or home so that I wouldn't be able to get to her or be with her.

As we left the school, my daughter was placed with the authorities to bring home and I had to leave by myself. I don't know how I made it home. My mind kept wondering on what I had missed and why hadn't I seen this coming. Still I hadn't heard my daughter speak.

As expected, he denied all initially and was removed and placed in custody.

After we arrived at home, it was determined I was not a threat to her and that I had no knowledge of these events. When my daughter finally was able to speak with me, what she revealed, I had no doubt in my mind that what she said was no fabrication. As she spoke, I began to relate to her experiences with him to that of my own. His mannerism, his demands of her, his verbiage. It was so familiar. I cried, cried until I couldn't cry anymore. I became literally sick with the thought of it. I held her so tight, she couldn't breathe. All this time, she had been trying to protect me. She put up with this abuse because of me. My God, what have I done. Not only was I abused, I introduced this man into my children's lives. What kind of mother am I? How could I have let this happen? Why didn't she come to me? Didn't she know that her happiness and safety came first? Where did I go wrong? Lord, please forgive me . . . . I became so angry!! I'll never forgive myself for this. I cried uncontrollably for what seemed like days. I couldn't speak to anyone. I wasn't eating. I couldn't even talk to her about this. I knew from what was already said that this happened. I didn't want to know anymore of the details.

Eventually, my daughter and I were placed in therapy while awaiting court. This forced us to see how all this came about.

Even after the initial outbreak of this, I still found it hard to discuss this with my daughter. I just wanted to erase all of this from my mind. I never was in denial, as some would call it. I just didn't want to discuss this particular subject. I was still

hurting and ashamed. Not for myself, but because of what I did and who it affected.

Victims Advocate placed us in therapy. This was so hard. My daughter was placed in a teen's group initially with other victims. I, on the other hand, was placed with indirect victims or parents/guardians of the victims. But this group was run by the abusers who had gone through the system and had been in therapy. I resented this. These abusers represented the same individual responsible for my being here.

After several years of therapy, depositions, court dates, continuances, and finally an actually hearing date; a plea bargain was settled on. He is currently serving time in our penal system with probation to follow. It was another few years before my daughter and I were released from therapy and to get on with our lives. What did this mean? Were we now conditioned in a manner that trust would not be

I've Been There...I Feel Your Pain

a virtue that we would expect to find in anybody? Were we now to live guarded and protected lives questioning every motive of those we had dealings with? The scars from this experience are still apparent and surface occasionally.

It took a good while before I could even look at another man. I was very uncomfortable just being in the same room with men. I wondered what kind of signal I was sending? What were they thinking? What hidden evil was lurking beneath the surface? What more could possibly happen?

I began to search myself. Who was I? What was I going to do now? I felt so alone and lonely. I wanted someone just to hold me tenderly and compassionately. I needed to feel love and be loved. I hated myself for what I was turning into. I hated the life that I was a part of. I hated the decisions that I had made and those that were hurt by them. I just wanted it to end. The pain seemed so unbearable. I had nothing to cling to. I felt as though I was hanging, literally, by a thread and losing my grip fast.

The only thing that kept me going on was the fact that my kids needed someone to take care of them. Lord knows I hadn't done a good job in the past. But I'd been given another chance.

You know, as I flashed back on the experiences in my life with the decisions that were made, I don't see what I would have changed. My motives were true and honest. These decisions were based on available knowledge and maturity and feelings at that time.

As coming to know Christ as my personal Savior who had delivered companion to grow old with.

As, what I thought, we grew closer we began to talk about marriage. After three (3) and a half years of what you would call courting, and settling down from this new high, I began to notice a few things. At this time, not enough to send out panic warnings so to speak (or maybe I should have taken a second look at things). He appeared very discrete and evasive when I wanted to meet members of his family and his children. He seemed to always have an excuse for that not happening. It wasn't that he wouldn't talk about them, I just couldn't meet them right now. Well, I allowed him to continue this for another couple of years and then I began to demand either to meet them or a good explanation as to why this was impossible. Well, finally, he started taking me around to his parents, sisters and brothers home in addition to taking me on vacation with him where I also met family in his home town. But still I hadn't met his children. I figured he had his reasons and I really didn't want to push it. Even though he had met everyone that was close to me which included my family and friends.

During this time, we both experienced sorrow with death in our families. I lost the only father I knew of, a sister and a step-brother the same year and a few months apart. It was nice to have a shoulder to lean on.

The subject of marriage came to the surface again. I almost immediately began to notice some change or discrepancies in the explanation or half stories he began to tell. As I'm planning this wedding and ordering invitations and setting up the occasion which, might I add, the date was selected by him, things still didn't seem right. What I mean by this is that he was saying. What I wanted to hear as far as each stage of the plan but it was missing his excitement or enthusiasm. Strangely, as I approached members of his family about our plans and this expected participation, I was met with reservations or disbelief. I didn't know what was happening. This should have been the happiest time for us, but it wasn't for him. In justifying his actions, I chalked it off to his age and maturity. I really wanted this to happen because I loved him so much. I continued to seek confirmation from him because by now, it was more than a plan. The only thing lacking was awaiting the day. We had starting receiving gifts, the office threw me a surprise shower in addition to my church group. I'm still confirming this verbal agreement because still something is missing.

Here it is now the day the wedding, the day if rehearsal I'm so excited. The day is coming. All of this will be behind me soon. Finally, a silver lining is seen the clouds and I get a personal visit from him the first thing in the morning. He came over acting very nervous and states "He can't go through with it"…I thought I was going to die on the spot. Words failed me. What was I hearing. I began to choke on my own breath. There was no real explanation. Why had he taken me through all this and then to pull the rug from up under me? This could have been stopped sooner. I was so hurt, angry ashamed. And humiliated. I asked him to leave. No, I demanded he get the hell out of my home. How could he do this to me?

It was three weeks before I would accept a call from him. I just couldn't figure out what went wrong. He had all the answers. It was important to me to know the whys. He really had nothing to offer in the line of an explanation. I didn't know what went wrong.

I did find out, without any help from him, that when we met he had been married only a year but living in separate residents. That's why there were no sign of female existence in his home. He was divorced only a year when we had set the original wedding date. From this information. I see why it was impossible to meet his family before. Pieces began to fall into place. But why couldn't he have

I've Been There...I Feel Your Pain

told me all this and allowed me to make a decision as to what I could do or should do?

I guess I am a glutton for punishment because he sweet talked his way back in my life making more promises if I allowed him some time to clear up obstacles that only he could do. So we continued to see each other. I told those that asked regarding the wedding that the wedding was postponed briefly.

After the time frame that was set for these changes had passed, another date to get married was scheduled. This time, we agreed to have a privately performed wedding. I only notified a few chosen friends. I didn't want ti explain things again to anyone if it didn't go through. At first, I thought maybe I was just being cautious, not fully recovered from the first set back. But the pattern appeared very familiar. Again, It didn't feel right. I wasn't sure he would go through with it. I was right. On the day we had set, that morning we spoke on the phone. Still there was no indication that he would renege. He said he was on his way to pick me up. Still I didn't get assurance in his voice so I decided to wait until he arrived before getting dressed. Within the hour, I received another phone call. He had stopped at a phone booth along the way to say he wasn't coming. The only relief I felt was that I didn't have to explain any of this to anyone. What a fool I had been to trust this man.

Right about now, I can't explain what I'm feeling. There appears to be a big whole in my chest where my heart use to be. Numbness took over my body. Who was this man? What in God's name had I done consciously or unconsciously to deserve this? What sin was I being punished for? Where is this man's heart?

I truly believed this man was the answer to my prayers. What more lord? I don't want to start all over with someone else. Too much has been invested. I'm getting to old for this. I guess at this point with his constant persistence, he insisted that I give him this last chance to prove me that his intention hadn't changed, that he still wanted to marry me. That he loved me. He was just confused. I began to justify being with him because I didn't want to try anything new. I was afraid that if I got involved with someone else it would be worse and I couldn't take anymore.

So yes, after all I've been through, I did start seeing him again. Taking one day at a time, not trusting, questioning any and all things. Well, after a while, he started in on marriage again and I just listened. He set a date again, I just listened. No hope no dreams, just a wait and see attitude. And then it happened. He showed up, got dressed and we proceeded to the nearest court house, still I was waiting for him to pull out. The next thing I remembered hearing was "husband and wife". Why wasn't I happy about this? Isn't this what I wanted? Why did I feel this wasn't a mutual union?

Those words took on a new meaning. Not like those mentioned in our current day Mr. Webster. The rules were different also. It wasn't an agreement between two people who loved each other and wanted to spend the rest of their lives together. It didn't mean 50/50. It was a marriage of convenience or obligation for one partner only. This was a little hard to justify in my mind when I had the root of what marriage meant in my heart. The struggles that transpired after this unity are beyond what one would ever comprehend. One should not have to try so hard to convince anyone of what their obligations are or should be. I felt like a sales person always. Selling myself, my attributes, trying to convince him that he made the best choice. On the other hand he wasn't giving us a chance. If you've ever been in a situation where things were not equal or balanced or at least at the same level or degree, you would understand where I was coming from. My love for him was so great, that I was denying myself of what I could be and trying to be what I thought he wanted from a companion, completely destroying who I was. Yet and still, this didn't seem to be enough. I've run out ideas. I'm tried of needing, hoping, wishing and being ignored, neglected, and denied. Am I not supposed to have feelings?

There were no sacrifices made by him. He didn't give up anything or make any changes. In essence, he only change my name.

The time that we shared initially began to diminish. Something else was occupying and taking over what could have been quality time for adjusting and setting goals for ourselves.

When it came to us, he didn't want to sit down and plan our future. He seemed to fight me on every turn as I tried to get closer to him. He never viewed us as a couple. He continues to pull away from me.

Today, nothing much has changed. As I wrote now. Its about 1:00 a.m. I still don't get much sleep and right now my husband's whereabouts are unknown to me, one more day before the dawning of a new year. One that I'm not too excited about.

As I set here reminiscing about my past, I'm not happy with the turn of events. No, that's putting it mildly. I'm very disappointed with myself and my life. I have no more fight left. I'm tired and I feel so all alone. I have nothing to show for all the years that I've been given.

I'm sorry, I wish things could have been different. It just seems like the choices I made were all bad. This is it for me. I have no more to give. My heart feels like its beating on borrowed time and time

I've Been There...I Feel Your Pain

is about to run out. I have this ache in my chest that seems to deepen with each breaths.

Well, I see now that things are just going to get worse. He doesn't want me and the demands of his other interest continues to drain all the life out of me. I still ask the appropriate questions. Why? What do I have to do? What more can I do? What can I change if I need to? If he would just let me know what's going on, I could try to resolve whatever the problem is. Is it me?

I through I would be able to rekindle those feelings I felt radiating from him when we first met. I through that just because I loved him that things would work out alright. Well, I was wrong, once again and alone as fate has always been.

When I look around, I see couples who appear to be happy or have a fulfilling life or I see individuals who seem to have it really going on. If not at the point in their lives where they want to be, at least working together to achieve the goals they have set for themselves. Then I began to compare or try to relate to them and I see I can't hold my own or feel like I'm just out of my league. Where did I go wrong? Was all the things I believed in wrong, like caring, forgiving, trust, honesty, love, tolerance, and patience? It's a life time of set backs and disappointments that pray on your tolerance and endurance that PUSH you to that decision. Its like a boiling point.

Well, it really doesn't matter now, you see, my time has run out.. I know now why a person gives up on life. THE PAIN IS JUST TO GREAT…..

NO! I WILL NOT BE A STATISTIC!!!!

WHERE DO I GO FROM HERE?

Have you ever felt you were at the cross road of your life and nothing has seemed to work before and now you have to make yet another one of those decisions as to which road to take? I've heard that if you were at rock bottom, you can only go up. Well, how do you turn things around?

Everything in life you've wanted you've had to fight for. Nothing came easy for you. You look around at those with whom you deal with daily and there life seems to be so much better than what you have.

I am not talking about envy or jealousy. But why does it seem the struggles are all mine.

There are times when I feel as though I'm the only survival on this planet and everyone around me are just puppets. They don't seem real. I feel life this is my life and no one else exists.

In life, in order to live, you have to make choices. Realizing that when the choices don't turn out the way you would have like them to, it could make making another decision very difficult.

All right, here I am at this fork. Do I take the right or the left road. What's in stake for me if I take a left? Let me tell you what I see. A very deserted road. Hardly worn. The leaves from the trees all appear to be dry and brown with the branches full of drooping moss. The area surrounding the trees look unkept with over grown thorns and weeds. There doesn't appear to be any form of life existing for as far as the eye can see. There is a definite stillness in this place.

I've Been There...I Feel Your Pain

Gosh, that was just the life I left behind me. I nurtured, loved, fertilized, cultivated, watered, and I still couldn't make it grow. What could I have done differently? Did I smother, overprotected, was I planting out of season? Tell me what? Was it just dead with no life left? Was it just a lost cause or just hopeless?

Now, on the other hand. As I look to the right… look at the birds flying high, the rabbits hiding in the bushes. The green leaves whistling in the breeze. The sun setting among the trees. The green grass so beautifully in place and the road, full of dredges worn from use. There is traffic going and coming.

Was there a secret that I wasn't told? Am I taking things to seriously? Did I miss something, something important like the key to a successful life?

In order to survive, I have to find the key. Where do I start? Do I review where I've been? Do I start from this point in my life? What if things don't get better? How will I know before I've gone too far if I've made the right decision? At what point do I stop?

One of Mr. Webster's descriptions of "Life" is:

> "The interval or amount of time during which anything exists or functions…Human activities, relationships, and interests collectively: A manner of activity or a characteristic of existence.."

First of all, I need to determine who I am and what is it I want out this life. I have to set my own goals long/short term. I need to love myself first. I need to place limits for myself to what's favorable and what is not.

I am here for a reason, and I don't believe it's to be a door mat. I've got to find out what works for me. I dove into this rut and now I have to dig my way out.

Since I can't solve the problems in my marriage all by myself, I must now put my energies in other facets of my. Rebuilding, restoring, replenishing, and replacing what has been damaged. The strength of my character has been altered temporarily and it may take some time to restore it, but it will be restored.

I believe that the experience I've encountered is the key and even though, I won't forget all that has happened, I may be able to use the experiences and turn this thing around in my favor. I don't know how, but there is a reason other than ignorance and stupidity that I had this cross to bare.

The attributes of my character are my positive strength. I won't decrease the degree of any of those traits, but use the knowledge I've obtained from my experiences and enhance what I have.

I don't know what I could have done in the past to change the outcome of what has happened. But as I set here, I think about the prayers I've prayed and how they been answered.

One needs to be careful of what they ask in prayer. Your answers to these prayers don't always come over night nor do they come automatically. A lot of times, we have to wait BUT the answers come right on time. Some are answered no, not yet, and of course yes.

On a usual day, in my talks with God I remember saying:

> Father God, in heaven… Thank you for this day and in my lying down at night, placing your angels to watch over me and my family.

to make. We know that you are not a forceful God but a forgiving and loving God.

Thank you for loving us in spite of our disobedience. Help us this day to not miss an opportunity to serve you. Help us not to be so involved in self that one lamb is neglected.

Give me patience and strength to endure satan's visit by means of those that we come across today or bring home when we meet again. Give me knowledge, wisdom and understanding of your will. Help me to recognize your will and that in which I must do.

Teach me the things that are pleasing in your sight, and always remind me of where my blessings come from.

Forgive me for my sins of omission and commission. If I've hurt one of your children in any way, Lord,

Thank you for our rising and in the use of all our faculties. Thank you for every breath we take and every step we make.

Thank you for the food on our table and the clothes on our backs. Thank you for the roof over our heads. Thank you for the job that you have allowed me to have and providing me a safe trip to and from.

Father, as we go in different directions throughout the day, Lord, protect and guide us as you have always done and if it is your will, bring us safely back to the fold.

Realizing Lord that the path has already been prepared we are asking you to open our spiritual eyes to accept the things that you would like for us to see. Give us that discerning spirit so that we can steer away for temptations place in out path. Because we realize Lord that the choices are ours

times have been too tough, he has been there to pick up the pieces.

Someone once told me that if you are not having troubles in your life, if you are not going through something that would cause you to bend your knees, if you are not going through something then you really need to be concerned. I realize now that God is not through with me yet. I'm being prepped for something great and I will have a story to tell that will have an impact on many.

I know that there is something I must do also. So I will be helping to prepare myself for what he has in store for me next. He has been teaching me all alone that I am his child. I can only put my trust in him and he will deliver me. Carnal man/woman will only fail me, and that the experiences, without him, drain my existence. Man can't give me the desires of my heart. The love that I shared please allow me in my life to retract and not be too proud to apologize. Help self to decrease and you increase in my life. Humble me father so that I may see spiritually, the needs of my brothers and sisters in Christ. I love you and need you in my life. Take control, in the name of Jesus, I am your instrument. Use me. In the name of your son, Jesus Christ, Amen.

As, I look at these words, I know now why,… I asked for patience and he taught me how through my experiences to be patient and wait. I asked for deliverance and I had to go through something to be delivered. I asked for deliverance and I had to be go through something to be delivered. I asked to be humble, I needed to see myself as I was. I asked to view through his eyes and I was make to see the pain he endured in his walks. I asked him to teach me. These are the ways that I have been taught. He has always been there and when

is agape. Way and beyond the love that any man can offer or understand.

So I really didn't lose anything, because my father is rich in houses and land. He holds the wealth of the world in his hand. So even though I lost my maternal mother and paternal/biological father in which I really didn't know my father in heaven has been watching over me and he has great plans for me.

So to all those who had and played a role in my life that made an impact on where I am today, I say thank you. Thank you for your role in my life. HEY, I REALLY DID HAD A LIFE…

www.ingramcontent.com/pod-product-compliance
Lightning Source LLC
LaVergne TN
LVHW040202080526
838202LV00042B/3285